Etiquette For The Socially Savvy Teen

ETIQUETTE FOR THE SOCIALLY SAVVY TEEN

Life Skills for All Situations

By Rebecca Black

CELESTIAL ARC PUBLISHING

Copyright © 2012 Rebecca Black
All rights reserved.

Revised 2019. Third Edition

CELESTIAL ARC PUBLISHING

ISBN-10: 1544899327
ISBN-13: 978-1544899329

DEDICATION

To my dearest friend and loving husband Walker Black. You have been my most ardent supporter and the very best editor a writer can have.

CONTENTS

Introduction 13
Chapter One: The Basics 15
    Becoming Socially Savvy 16
    Developing Healthy Relationships 17
        Family Relationships 17
    Safety 19
        When You Are Away From Home 19
        When You Are at Home 19
    Siblings 22
    Guests 24
    How to Treat Hired Help 25
    Sharing Common Rooms & Items 26
        Practice for Future College Students 26
    Borrowing the Family Car 28
    Tough Times 29
        Divorce 29
        Parental Dating 29
        Remarriage 30
        Alcohol and Drugs 30
        Abusive Behavior 30
        Death or Suicide 30
    Time to Use the Information 32

Chapter Two: Communication Skills 33
Non-Verbal Communication 34
- Self-Confidence 34
- Appearances 35
- Proper Hygiene 36
- Attire 36

Verbal Communication 38
- Proper Introductions and Greetings 38
- Rules of Introductions 38
- Starting a Conversation 39
- Listen to Yourself 40
- Quiet 40

Telephone Etiquette 41
- Safety 43
- Voice Mail/Landline Answering Machines 43

Electronic Communication 45
- Cellphone Text Messaging 45
- Email and Instant Messaging 46
- Cellphone Etiquette 47

Social Networking 49

Written Communication 50
- Envelope 51
- The Correct Forms of Address 51
- Letters to Government Officials 53

    Formal Invitations 53

    Informal Invitation 54

    Thank You Note 55

    Condolence Note 55

Time to Use the Information 56

Chapter Three: Polite Behavior in Shared Spaces 57

What Are Shared Spaces? 58

    Expected Behavior 58

Sporting Events 62

Dining Out 63

Graduation 65

    Note 65

Special Considerations 66

What makes us popular? 67

Time to Use the Information 68

Chapter Four: Organizational Skills 69

Are You Organized? 70

Organizational Tools 71

    Clean Your Room! 72

    Academic Planners and Notebooks 73

    The Big Project 74

Stay Organized at Home 76

Master Calendar 78

Schedule Your Time 80

Where do you work? When?	81
Preparing for Tomorrow	82
Goal Setting	83
Time to Use the Information	84
Chapter Five: Dating Etiquette	**85**
Changes in Dating Etiquette	86
Body Language & Being our Best	87
Conversational Skills	90
Taboo Topics for First Dates	92
How to Meet Your Date	94
Asking for the Date	95
The Date	97
A Note to the Men	97
A Note to the Ladies	99
A Primer on Sliding Out of a Car Seat	101
Dating Do (s) and Don't (s)	102
Ideas for a Great Date	103
Bad dates	103
Time to Use the Information	104
Chapter Six: Prom Etiquette	**105**
Enjoying Your Prom	105
Planning for The Prom	106
Formal or Semi-formal	107
Tuxes	108

Flowers	109
The Dinner	110
The Dance	111
After the Dance parties	111
Table Manners Primer	112
Rules to Remember	112
Napkin Rules	113
Bread and Rolls	113
Do Not	114
Prom Reminders	115
Ladies	115
Gentlemen	116
Gentlemen and Ladies	116
Frequently Asked Questions	117
Time to Use the Information	118
Chapter Seven: Business Etiquette	119
Where to Begin?	120
How to Acquire the Job	121
Resume Information	121
Filling out Applications	122
Setting up the Interview	123
The Interview	124
Be Prepared	125
Be Honest	125

Thank the Interviewer 125
Once you have the Job.. 126
Considerations 126
Difficult Situations.. 128
Honesty and Integrity 130
Office Politics 132
Negative Office Politics... 133
Netiquette 136
Become an Entrepreneur 138
Time to Use the Information.. 140
Answers To Quiz Questions 141
Your Author 147

INTRODUCTION

I realize that there are many different types of family these days. You may not live with a mother and a father. You may be living with a guardian, or other family member. For this book, I will be using the word parents often because it is less cumbersome for readers to read one word rather than several. I hope this does not offend.

This book begins with basic manners and becoming a socially savvy person. I repeat this theme throughout the entire book, especially while discussing dating, prom and business etiquette. After all, we need to have the very best manners and people skills in all these situations.

As you read on, you will also learn how to build healthy relationships. This includes how to treat guests and hired help. Additionally, we also explore many touchy issues, like borrowing the family car. As you progress further through the book, I address more specific behaviors such as organizational skills, dating, prom and business etiquette.

Expected behavior is another common theme sprinkled throughout the book. It is my most sincere hope that when you finish this book, you feel prepared for most any situation because you know what is expected of you. Thus, you will feel comfortable in all situations.

CHAPTER ONE

THE BASICS

BECOMING SOCIALLY SAVVY

Have you noticed the person who always knows what to do, how to stand, and can make friends with anyone? Sure, you have. This person knows proper etiquette, which is the protocol we use in any given situation. Let's consider the snowboarder.

The snowboarder knows what uniform he should wear and he knows what his tools are—his snowboard. In *all* situations, we need to know what the proper etiquette (or protocol) should be in order to feel comfortable with our surroundings.

What are manners? Basically, it is a set of behaviors. We are to treat others as we wish to be treated. To do this we act out of **courtesy, kindness**, and **respect**.

Knowledge of proper etiquette and good manners assists you in succeeding in all the endeavors you choose for your life. This knowledge leads to good social skills, which are essential in developing the necessary business skills that we call, 'people' skills. To climb up that career-ladder and to cultivate healthy relationships in all facets of our lives we must have the *very* best people skills.

DEVELOPING HEALTHY RELATIONSHIPS

What type of relationship do you want to have with your friends? Silly question isn't it. Of course, we all want to have good relationships with our friends. However, we learn how to treat others by our relationships with our family at home.

FAMILY RELATIONSHIPS

Did you know that parents are not obligated to provide much more than adequate clothing, food, and lodging for you? In fact, there is no law that states that they must buy you *things*, or to even be nice. Thus, everything they do for you is out of their love for you, even when they discipline you for stepping outside your boundaries.

Knowing this, how do you demonstrate to your family that you care for them? What do you do to contribute? Do you pick up the newspaper in the morning? If both parents work, do you ask if you could cook dinner that night? Clean up after yourself? Perhaps you can make a list of ways that you can contribute more. Because remember, the behavior you use at home and the relationships you develop with family members will assist you in cultivating better friendships.

Communication is imperative in all our relationships. Once again, we begin at home to learn better communication skills. When you are upset, talk to your parents using the word **, I** instead of **you**, or it sounds like blaming. To say, "I am upset about my chores," sounds much better than, "You make me upset giving me so many chores."

Keep parents informed of the events in your life, like when you make new friends or have difficult classes. Parents are so busy trying to make everyone's lives perfect that they forget to slow down and listen. You may need to initiate the dialogue.

Also, inform parents of your schedule. The perfect tool is a master calendar. A master calendar lists everyone's schedule, including birthdays, doctor appointments, and test dates—everything that would affect someone else's schedule.

Say that you have an important test this Friday. If this were listed on the calendar, everyone would know that you need to study Thursday night and nothing else would be scheduled during that time. This calendar should be accessible to everyone.

For more information about 'Master Calendars,' please read the *Organizational Skills* chapter.

Note:
- Some cellphone calendar programs do this for us now.

SAFETY

Respecting your parents includes trying to stay safe, as to reduce their concern. So consider all of the ways you can increase your safety at home and away. This is not only important because, of course, you want to be safe, but also because you wouldn't want others to worry about you. Please consider this list.

WHEN YOU ARE AWAY FROM HOME

Make sure your cellphone is charged.

You just may need to call them in an emergency.

Do you have your house key?

You may not be the first out of the house that day, but you may be the first to return—have your house key on you.

Never ride with strangers.

This seems like a no-brainer. Nevertheless, sometimes we don't take situations as seriously as we should. That person you just met through a friend is still a stranger.

WHEN YOU ARE AT HOME

Pick up the mail and newspaper.

If there are newspapers lying out front, it could appear as an invitation to a burglar—as if no one is home. Moreover, you don't want someone getting your mail, giving them access to your personal information.

Lock all the doors.

This is a very simple rule often over-looked, but is vitally important. Check your windows also.

Never open the door for someone you don't know.

If you don't know the person, don't open the door. Sometimes we think that we must open the door when someone knocks because it is the 'polite' thing to do. Safety matters more.

Program important numbers as speed-dial on cellphones or keep a list nearby.

You never know when an emergency may occur. When that time arrives, you may be too nervous to remember phone numbers. So, keep these handy. Of course, we all know 911!

Don't go into your home if something looks suspicious.

Seems like another no-brainer, but again we assume that we can handle anything or think we are being silly when we are afraid. If you suspect anything is out of place, don't go into your home. The police are there to help you. Call from a safe location and they will ensure that your home is safe to enter.

Keep your parents informed of every time you leave.

Even if you are going next door, let your parents know so they won't worry. I once had a student who was going to the store on her bike. Her parents were at work and she didn't tell them where she was going. She fell into a ditch, broke her leg and laid there for hours because no one knew where she was.

Never take new medication when parents are not present.

Even over-the-counter drugs that seem safe may not be safe for you. Take for example a story from my childhood. Around the age of 14 years old, I woke up one morning not feeling well. I was dizzy and nauseous, but still wanted to go to school. I couldn't ask my parents for help because both of them had already left for work.

I decided to search our medicine cabinet for something to make me feel better. After reading labels of all the bottles, I found one for motion sickness. The label stated that it helps eliminate nausea and dizziness associated with motion sickness—close enough for me. I took one pill and I'm off to school.

During first period class, I felt as if I was going to pass out. My teacher took me aside and through his questioning, we found that the pill made me sick. It turned out that I am hypoglycemic. Silly me; I just needed food.

SIBLINGS

Do you have siblings? How do all of you get along?

As this world becomes increasingly crowded every day, we are forced to interact with those we don't know well. Let's learn how to develop healthy relationships with all we encounter through our struggles with our brothers and sisters.

One common problem with siblings is jealousy. I remember thinking that my sister was so lucky and got more than I did because she was much prettier than I was. Funny, as we talk now, she thought the same thing about me. We could have avoided many of our problems by communicating better. You can too.

Privacy can also be a serious issue. Respect their diaries by never reading them. Moreover, for heaven's sake, please don't post it on the Internet. When his or her door is closed, knock before entering. When they receive phone calls, do not listen in or yell in the background. Remember, they could do the same when your friends call.

GUESTS

When you have guests visit you, please introduce them to your parents properly. Younger people are always introduced to older. Consequently, you would introduce your friend to your parent. For example, "Mother, I would like to introduce to you, my friend from school, Juan Gutierrez." "Juan, this is my mother, Mrs. James."

Treat your friends as special. This means that you would give them the best chair, let them choose the first movie or game, and allow them to make the decision between pizza and hot dogs. Inform them which rooms are off limits and other rules that you live by. You wouldn't want your friend to be embarrassed by waking your father who works nights, would you?

When your parents have guests, be on your best behavior. If you are sitting and the guest arrives, greet that person properly. This is great practice for those times that you will meet representatives from companies at career fairs in your near future.

If meeting the guest for the first time, turn the television or games down or off, stand, shake hands when that person extends hers, and say that it is nice to meet her.

HOW TO TREAT HIRED HELP

If you live in a household that retains some type of hired help, such as an in-home nanny, housekeeper, gardener, or even a dog walker, treat that person with respect. That person is hired to do a specific job so we shouldn't ask for extra help with duties outside of that person's job description.

In addition, never talk down to this person just because your family is paying him or her to provide a service for you. No one is lower or less important than another person is. We are all on the same level.

SHARING COMMON ROOMS & ITEMS

PRACTICE FOR FUTURE COLLEGE STUDENTS

Must you share a room? Many of us do or have in the past. I remember sharing a room with my messy little sister for years. I didn't like it much. However, when I finally received my own room – which I thought would be so great because I could keep it clean and decorate it just the way I wanted – I was lonely. I missed my messy little sister.

Space is at a premium when we share a room, so respect each other's space and property. This is wonderful practice for your future college-dorm days.

Discuss how you will share storage, television and all other shared items. The noise from electronics can be especially obnoxious at times. Agree on neatness from the very beginning and stick to your agreement. Finally, do not borrow anything without asking.

There are common rooms in your home and future dorms that require special attention, such as your present family room and kitchen. Please leave each room the way you found it or better. Pick up wrappers and soda cans after your friends leave.

Don't eat food that appears as if it could be for a special occasion without asking. So, if you find a beautiful cake in the refrigerator, ask first before diving in.

Also, do your dishes. No one should have to clean up after you. Take care of your own wet towels. Ask what you should do with these and follow directions.

Clean the tub out and wipe down the shower walls. It is much easier to keep watermarks off shower walls if we dry them after each use. Moreover, don't hog the bathroom. We all share.

Share appliances with those in your household, always keeping them in good condition. So, before using the washer and dryer, ask for instruction. Additionally, you should be doing your own laundry. You have more control over how your clothes appear and you are contributing to the household chores.

Clean your messes in the microwave and refrigerator. Ask for instructions for the dishwasher, and rinse dishes before loading them.

Electronics? Learn how to use the shared television, computer, Blu-ray player, and stereo. You may wish to ask to read the owner's manuals. Share usage of these items and be aware of sound levels. Remember that others may want quiet. Take special care of small items such as cameras, cellphones, etc. Avoid dropping or misplacing them and return to where you found them. They will last longer. Finally, ask before borrowing any of these and return them in as good a condition as you found them

Does everyone in your home share all of these items and rooms like this? What could be improved?

BORROWING THE FAMILY CAR

A car is expensive to buy, to insure, and to maintain, so keep this in mind when asking to borrow the family vehicle. Offer to trade a waxing, to run errands or chauffeuring a sibling for the opportunity to borrow the car. This will usually endear you to your parents, which is always a great idea.

Also, ask in advance, not last minute. Never take the vehicle without asking. This could get you in very hot water. Obey the law, with an emphasis on following all speed limits.

Always return the car in good or better condition than you borrowed it.

Finally, except no for an answer; as there is not anything more tiring for a parent than whining.

TOUGH TIMES

Sometimes families have problems and we need to ask ourselves how we are behaving. It is easy to become part of the problem because we are distressed also. After all you are leaving childhood behind, moving into adulthood and rules of the road are not quite clear at times.

These difficult situations seem to be the most common, yet the most difficult for most of us:

DIVORCE

Husbands and wives divorce each other not their children. I realize that it seems as if you are in the middle of it, but this is a problem between your parents. Talk to each of your parents about your future when each is calm. If you cannot find a time, create one; ask when a time will be appropriate. Always attempt to stay neutral.

PARENTAL DATING

How is the dating world treating you? Do you get nervous? Always know what to do? Well, your parent is no different. It is difficult at all ages. So if one or both parents begin to venture into the dating world, please be patient. It doesn't mean that you are no longer important or this person is going to be part of your life. Dating is merely testing each person to find a match.

REMARRIAGE

Yikes! Your parents are remarrying. This can be stressful—new parents, new siblings. Where will you fit in? Remind yourself to treat others as you wish to be treated. Moreover, try to be open-minded. You don't have to adopt them as family, yet. Just try to blend. In addition, keep a line of communication open with your parent. Be honest about your feelings.

ALCOHOL AND DRUGS

Many of us have family members who have a problem with substance abuse. If you are one of us, seek help from Al-Anon, a support group that will help you understand the addiction and not become a partner in it. I hope that your family member will seek help also. Help is free and easily accessible.

ABUSIVE BEHAVIOR

Speak up! Find an adult you trust, one who will take you seriously. Perhaps a counselor or a teacher could help. *Please* seek help. Always remember that it is not your fault.

DEATH OR SUICIDE

Have you had a recent loss? It is a very trying time of life. You may feel anger, shock, denial, guilt, and hopefully soon acceptance. There are books that might help you through the rough spots, but talking with others will help also. Please ask for help. Grieving takes time; don't feel as if you have to get over it quickly.

Note

There are crisis lines available for just about every crisis. If you are unsure about whom to call for help, ask someone you trust.

TIME TO USE THE INFORMATION

1) What will you do to help more around the house?
   _____
   _____

2) How will you ensure you are safe when away from the house?
   _____
   _____

3) How can you be a better host to guests?
   _____
   _____

CHAPTER TWO

COMMUNICATION SKILLS

NON-VERBAL COMMUNICATION

We begin our discussion of communication skills with non-verbal communication, which is basically body language. Your posture speaks volumes about how you feel about yourself and your surroundings. How might others perceive you if you slouch or slump? When you stoop, with your head down making no eye contact, others will view you as insecure. Yet, if you walk tall with your head up and make good eye contact, others will view you as self-assured.

Aristotle stated, "People are virtuous because they act rightly." ...which means, that we do the right thing and then we become that virtuous person. How right he was. It is now widely known that our actions precede how we view ourselves. This is because others react to our behavior and actions.

SELF-CONFIDENCE

Once upon a time not too long ago, a college professor asked his students to participate in a research study as part of their grade. He separated his students into groups and asked his students of psychology to pretend for a period of time to be popular, to be unpopular, and to be the average Joe or Jane.

At the end of the time-period, those who pretended to be popular were; those who pretended to be unpopular were, and those who pretended to be the average Joes/Janes were. What does this study illustrate? This tells us that people believe what they see. If we behave in a certain way, those around us believe it.

Actions precede feelings. In fact, many psychologists now concur. Therefore, if we pretend that we are self-confident and suave, others will notice, believe, and treat us as if we are; we mentally absorb this and become the person others believe we are. We will then become that person.

Also important is how we sit. When wearing slacks, females may cross one knee over another. Young men may also cross their legs. With skirts, females should cross their ankles because skirts ride up and may become too short. However, no one should sit with legs open! This appears as if the person has been riding a horse for a month!

Note

Do not smack gum! It is noisy and very unattractive.

Each of us has a personal space, a buffer that we consider ours. Therefore, we must honor everyone's personal space by not entering it.

APPEARANCES

You have less than thirty seconds to make the first impression. Yes, it is true. Others judge you by your appearance in just a few seconds. So, always ask yourself, "What impression am I making?"

PROPER HYGIENE

Have you had to sit next to someone with questionable hygiene? Not very pleasant, is it?

Proper hygiene is crucial. Someone who is smelly is not someone we tend to gravitate toward, so always consider your hygiene. It's best not to be that smelly person. Therefore, bathe daily, which also includes brushing our teeth, and washing our hair.

In fact, proper hygiene is so important, one city created a hygiene mandate. A city official in a certain Tennessee city states that one smelly employee is responsible for a new policy that requires all city employees to smell nice when at work. The policy reads that no employee shall have an odor generally offensive to others when reporting to work. An offensive body odor may result from a lack of good hygiene, from an excessive application of a fragrant aftershave or cologne or from another cause.

No, this is no joke, as exposure to a person who smells is no joke. Never be that smelly person.

ATTIRE

Consider how are you dressed, as we know we are judged by how we look. Remember, you only have one chance to make a first impression.

Consider, as well, those times that it may be important to look your best. How about an interview, a relative's party, a nice restaurant? Absolutely! So, scrutinize your image in the mirror before leaving the house.

For those special occasions, avoid stomach revealing, tight fitting tops, short skirts, shorts, pants that hang around the lower hips and flip-flops.

Note

Please no hats indoors! This includes baseball hats.

VERBAL COMMUNICATION

Communication is imperative in all our relationships. Can you imagine a good relationship with your boyfriend or girlfriend without good communication? It wouldn't last long would it. Nevertheless, what do you consider the most important component of communication? If you guessed listening, you are correct. We need to listen to everyone when he or she speaks. Listen attentively.

PROPER INTRODUCTIONS AND GREETINGS

We cannot begin a relationship without being introduced. Introductions and greetings are essential. If you are introducing yourself, stand, extend your hand and say, "Hello my name is first and last name" and when the person says his or her name repeat it and say that it is nice to meet her. This will help you remember her name.

Please introduce others by mentioning first and last names with a bit of information about them.

RULES OF INTRODUCTIONS

There is a hierarchy for introducing one to another. Younger people are introduced to their elders: Mom, "This is my college roommate Juan Gutierrez." Juan, "This is my mother, Jacklyn Crowder." Introduce guests to hosts. Additionally, as a sign of respect, introduce people to others with higher standings such as senator, governor, mayor, clergy, etc... Finally, please avoid introducing anyone as your friend unless introducing all as friends, because that implies the other person may not be your friend.

STARTING A CONVERSATION

Becoming a good conversationalist is not impossible; it just requires practice. Start with the information given to you. Ask how the person knows a common friend. Make comments such as, "Tell me about yourself."

Listen to what he or she says and follow up with the theme. So, if this person is talking about golf, ask specific questions about golf and golfing.

Mention music that may be playing in the background. Inquire about that person's preferences.

Avoid, however, ethnic jokes, slurs, politics, and religion. These topics can create a negative atmosphere. Also, avoid gossip. Gossip is a destructive force that can ruin relationships. If you were to gossip about someone, the person hearing it may wonder what you say behind his or her back.

Don't reveal too much personal information in the beginning of your relationship. You may have the neighborhood gossip telling everyone how you sing to your cat every morning. And always, remember your manners.

LISTEN TO YOURSELF

Do you whine? Use the same words repeatedly? Cuss? Grunt? All these noises will define you to others. Listen carefully to all the noise you make and adjust the volume.

QUIET

Quiet is expected in most public places, such as waiting rooms, busses and libraries. Why is this so? Well, in most of these places we wish to think and reflect in quiet. Thus, if we make noise by talking excessively or loudly, we affect others' personal space. We all have a space around us that includes a quiet quotient. We should respect this.

TELEPHONE ETIQUETTE

Many do not use a landline telephone anymore. For those who do, the following information is for you. Please be mindful of the length of your calls if you share a phone. Identify yourself when you make a call. Therefore, if you call your friend Joe, identify yourself and tell him or her whom you are calling. For example, "Hello, my name is John Abernathy, calling for Joe. May I speak to him please?"

Do not identify yourself when someone calls you. This may seem rude to some, but we should consider our safety first. Why would someone have to know your name if he is calling you? If someone asks for your name, return the request with, "With whom do you wish to speak?"

Additionally, do not call someone too often or before 8 am or after 9 pm.

It is perfectly appropriate for young ladies to call young men these days; it is no longer considered improper. In addition, always ask if this is a good time to talk.

If you dial a wrong number, apologize and check the number called.

Always sound interested in what the caller is talking about and do not do anything else while the caller is talking. Often my sister will be doing the dishes or some other chore while we are talking. I'm left wondering if she is listening to me at all.

Moreover, excuse yourself to the caller when talking to someone else in the room. It is irritating to the caller to wonder to whom you are talking. Do not disturb those around you while you are on the phone, so take your call into another room.

Do not eat while on the phone. Your caller should feel as if he or she is important.

Always remember call waiting rules. When you talk to someone on the phone and know that you must check all in-coming calls, alert your caller at the beginning of the call. Check the second call when you are beeped. Inform the second caller that you are conversing with caller number one and will return his or her call soon; ask when would be a good time. Then return to the first caller.

If this is an emergency or an out-of-town call, politely inform your first caller and ask when would be a good time to return the call.

Ask for the caller's first and last name, plus the proper spelling when taking phone messages. In the past I have only asked for the caller's first name and when I returned the call, I found that there were three people with the same name working in that office.

Ask for the caller's phone number; ask when the call may be returned and the purpose of the call.

When you wish to use someone else's landline phone, ask first. Keep those calls brief and offer to pay for the calls.

SAFETY

As mentioned earlier in this book, always have emergency numbers handy. You may become too nervous to remember important numbers during an emergency. In addition, call police if you think you have an intruder. Police *want* you to call; please do not feel embarrassed. Yep, I've mentioned this before, but it's worth repeating.

Hang up if you receive an obscene or threatening phone call.

VOICE MAIL/LANDLINE ANSWERING MACHINES

There is specific etiquette involved with messages left for others—when using a landline answering machine—and soliciting messages from callers. Here are the most important rules.

Return messages as quickly as possible. It is frustrating to the caller to wait around for a response.

Do not record an offensive announcement on your answering machine or voice mail. Consider all who may be calling. I had a young male client not too long ago, whose grandmother called and received an earful when she only reached the family's answering machine. He thought he was being funny. No one else viewed it in the same light.

Never leave an offensive message. You never know who will be listening. Moreover, if there is a message for someone living with you, do not erase it. Inform that person that there is a message for him. If the message is for a person not living in the home, say it is a wrong number and inform that person if possible.

ELECTRONIC COMMUNICATION

Today, electronic communication is pervasive. Text messaging has become nearly as popular as email because it is fun, quick, and effective. Nevertheless, we need to observe some etiquette. We would not want to be rude to those with whom we communicate.

CELLPHONE TEXT MESSAGING

Do not text someone, while in the company of another.

- It is considered as rude as taking a voice call.

Text messaging is informal.

- Do not use it for formal invitations.

Do not dissolve a relationship using text messaging.

Be patient while waiting for a reply.

- Watch your frustration level.
- Your recipient may not be as adept at texting as you.

Be aware of your tone.
- Your message can be misinterpreted entirely. Reread your messages carefully.

Texting while driving is dangerous.
- There is no possible way anyone can watch the road and text at the same time.

Watch your slang.
- Yes, this is an informal form of communication, but the slang can become part of your everyday language.
- Stay on top of your game with proper grammar.

Texting can be traced.
- Do not send messages that may be perceived as improper.

EMAIL AND INSTANT MESSAGING

Respond to your email as quickly as possible using good judgment in your language. Additionally, anyone can see your email; it is not private. Therefore, you would not want to write anything that you wouldn't want posted on a bulletin board.

Email is a form of writing, so always use good grammar, spelling, and tone.

Instant messaging can be an enjoyable activity; but is not private and sometimes is not safe, especially in the social networking world. Be careful. The cute 6'2", dark haired 17-year-old could be a 42-year-old man with a beer-belly and very bad habits.

If you Tweet or message someone on social networking sites – such as Facebook – always ask your recipient if he/she has the time to converse. I have friends who continually want to engage in a lengthy conversation on-line. My answer is always the same. I simply don't have time. Therefore, I appear off-line all day.

It is considered impolite to invite someone to join an instant-messaging conversation that is ongoing without asking the others who are conversing first.

Like email, don't use all capital letters to type your message; it appears as shouting at your recipient. If your recipient does not respond, don't repeatedly message him. Consider that person busy. In addition, do not enter into more than three conversations at one time. You won't be able to give anyone your undivided attention.

CELLPHONE ETIQUETTE

Do

- Remove your Blue Tooth device when with others.

No Ringing

- In a restaurant and in a theater during a movie
- During a doctor/dental exam.
- During an interview.
- At the golf course.
- During a discussion.

- In the library, a place of worship, in court, and in hospitals.

Avoid Conversing

- In every situation mentioned above.
- While a checker in a store is ringing up your purchases.
- During a haircut or styling.

Avoid loud melodic ringing in public places

SOCIAL NETWORKING

Number One Rule

On social networking sites, or any other, never write anything you wouldn't say to another person face to face.

Avoid

- Cyber dumping
- Sharing personal information
- Posting racy or potentially embarrassing photos
- Posting hateful or untruthful gossip about others
- Using profanities or poor grammar

My book *Electronic Etiquette* is a great resource for learning more on this subject.

WRITTEN COMMUNICATION

When is the last time you sent a thank you card? ...a sympathy card? These niceties create lasting friendships and indicate to others that you are a polite, caring and socially adept person.

There is no substitution for a handwritten card sent via snail mail when it comes to thank you or sympathy card. For birthday cards, an e-card is considered passable but is still not on par with the 'real' thing. Moreover, we would never use email or an e-card for sympathy cards.

Choose nice stationary with playful colors for letters to family and friends. Choose neutral colors, gray, white, and cream for business letters. Use pen, not pencil for a more formal appearance. Always, type your business letters.

ENVELOPE

Mr. James Wilson

223 Adams Street

Jackson, Mississippi 23343

                    Ms. Elizabeth Jones

                    588 Washington Road

                    Claremont, Louisiana 22398

THE CORRECT FORMS OF ADDRESS

Boys under 7

- Master John Smith
- Dear John

Boys 7-18

- John Smith
- Dear John

Man 18 or over

- Mr. John Smith
- Dear Mr. Smith or Dear John

Unmarried girl
- Miss/Ms. Jane Jones
- Dear Jane or Dear Miss/Ms Jones

Woman
- Ms. Jane Jones
- Dear Ms. Jones

Married
- Mrs./Ms. Jane Jones
- Dear Mrs./Ms. Jones

Divorced
- Mrs./Ms. Jane Jones
- Dear Mrs./Ms. Jones

Widowed
- Mrs. John Jones
- Dear Mrs. Jones

LETTERS TO GOVERNMENT OFFICIALS

The Letter

123 Cherry Lane

Sonoma, California 94532

Date

Dear Senator Boxer:

Respectfully,

Me

The Envelope

The Honorable Barbara Boxer

112 Hart Building

Washington, DC 20510

FORMAL INVITATIONS

Mr. and Mrs. Juan Ortiz

request the pleasure of your company

on Sunday, the twentieth of June

at three o'clock

R.S.V.P.

35 Clark Place

Joy Land, Oregon

This should be mailed at least six weeks in advance.

The Response

Ms. Rebecca Black

accepts with pleasure

Or

regrets that she is unable to accept

your kind invitation

for

Sunday, the twentieth of June

INFORMAL INVITATION

Birthday Party

Shannon Brown

Date

2 P.M. to 5 P.M.

THANK YOU NOTE

Date

Dear Aunt Jane,

    I love my new chessboard; thank you. I have already beaten my dad twice. Maybe we can play a game the next time you come to visit.

See you soon.

Love,

Peggy

CONDOLENCE NOTE

Date

Dear Frank,

    I just learned of the death of your mother. I know how much she meant to you, so this must be very difficult for you. Please accept my deepest sympathies and know that I am always thinking of you. Please call if there is anything I can do.

Sincerely,

Jane Drummond

TIME TO USE THE INFORMATION

1) What would you wear to a nice restaurant?
   _____
   _____

2) How will you begin a conversation?
   _____
   _____

3) How will you use a cellphone politely?
   _____
   _____

CHAPTER THREE

POLITE BEHAVIOR IN SHARED SPACES

WHAT ARE SHARED SPACES?

Shared spaces are places that we share with the public at large, such as schools, libraries, stores, buses, trains, parks, etc. Can you think of some?

EXPECTED BEHAVIOR

A certain type of behavior is expected in these public or shared spaces. We begin by considering our basic 'good manners' when we are in public; treating others as we wish to be treated.

Consequently, let's not jump to conclusions about others. That 'nerdish' looking guy in front of you in line just may be the next Bill Gates. Moreover, because people do jump to conclusions about others, we should always think about how our behavior may influence other people's view of us before they even get to know us.

Always remember that our behavior affects those around us. What we do in our space affects others. Therefore, we need to revisit our posture.

Why is it so important? If you remember from the first chapter, your posture directly affects how others perceive you. Consequently, if you appear as a confident person, standing tall, looking forward, smiling, and making eye contact, others will believe that you are that confident person.

Always obey the rules posted at malls, parks, zoos, etc. This means no loitering, no skateboards, and no visiting parks after 10 pm. Hey, you shouldn't be out that late anyway.

There is an etiquette involved when it comes to elevators. If the elevator is crowded, the persons closest to the door exit first. Gender is not an issue in this case. However, if it is not crowded, women and girls enter and leave first. The one exception is if there are elderly onboard. Older people are considered most important-- we give those much older than ourselves respect. The person closest to the "Door Open" button should hold it until everyone who wants out is out and those who want in are in.

We all know that we should hold the door for people, but for whom and when? We should hold the door for someone carrying packages, for a mother with a stroller and anyone needing assistance, such as someone in a wheelchair. Men should hold doors for women.

It is a gentlemanly gesture. Finally, we should hold the door for anyone close behind us. Can you imagine a door closing in *your* face?

Because we want to demonstrate our respect for those around us we should consider a few rules.

Be on time for appointments.

When we are late for an appointment, it is as if we are saying that our time is more valuable than their time.

Settle in before a show begins.

We should be seated in our seats, coats removed, packages of snacks opened, and not be rustling around when the show begins. We don't want to disturb those around us by making any kind of noise.

Turn off electronic equipment, especially cell phones.

It is irritating to most others to have to listen to someone else's phone conversation. Plus, to hear a cell phone ring during a movie is very disturbing.

Quiet

Most people want quiet in shared spaces. People want to enjoy the space without someone else interrupting their peace with loud voices.

Stay in your space.

Imagine sitting in a restaurant with those little tables and benches along a wall. You are on the bench. You have very little space between you and the next person sitting in front of her table. Be very conscious of how you use your space. Where are your jacket, purse, and backpack?

Wear appropriate clothing.

There are times when it is best to dress up. We realize that we need to dress up when our parents say we must. However, there are times we should dress up just because it is the correct thing to do, such as when a relative comes to visit. You would also want to dress up when meeting new people, including a boy/girlfriend's parents, visiting a restaurant, ballet, and a play.

Watch your temper and language.

There are times that we feel angry. Please remember that your anger is yours and that no one can 'make' you angry. Learn how to control it and not allow it to control you.

SPORTING EVENTS

Watch your temper while attending a sporting event. It is disconcerting to watch many of the sporting events on television these days and watch players and fans fighting. This is simply infantile, socially inept behavior. Don't become a part of it. It is just a game—that is all, nothing more.

Be a good sport while participating. Nothing sours a game faster than some loud mouth yelling at the umpire, or referee.

Admit errors with a smile. We all make mistakes. How we react to our mistakes helps make us the quality people we wish to be.

Be sincere when offering comments, such as "It always bothers me too when I miss the ball."

Note

Our behavior in airports, on airplanes, in buses and trains is of concern also. We need to be very conscious about our voice level and actions.

Remember, our behavior affects other's space.

DINING OUT

You wouldn't want to be embarrassed or embarrass those around you while dining in a restaurant.

So let's discuss some restaurant etiquette beginning with a little story.

While dining out, my husband and I witnessed a young boy, approximately ten, playing soccer with a straw while his father was sitting only a few feet away from him. No kidding. It seemed as if he was trying to see how high he could kick it. I could almost hear the cheers of the crowd.

While Father saw what Mr. Soccer was doing, I don't believe he found fault in his son's actions, as he did nothing. I thought, "What a terrible loss of a teachable moment". Dad should have known that a restaurant is no place for a soccer game.

When we visit a restaurant, any type of restaurant, we are just visiting. We need to show respect for property, other diners and for those who work there. Please treat the waitstaff with respect; they are people, not just fixtures.

A reservation at a restaurant is a promise of arrival, so, punctuality is paramount. It is disrespectful to the proprietors if you waste their time.

If you have not made a reservation, please ask politely for inclusion.

Pushy, elitist behavior or attitudes are rude and not acceptable behavior no matter how important this dinner may be.

GRADUATION

Graduation is an exciting time, so plan ahead by first deciding to graduate. If family members need to travel, inform them very early of your graduation date. Spend special time, perhaps a lunch, with those who cannot attend.

If you want a limo, earn money throughout the year to pay for it. Call for rates from several sources and share with a few friends.

You are required to attend graduation rehearsals. This is a once in a lifetime event, so enjoy each component of the activity. Dress and act appropriately, which means that you should wear dressy clothing under your gown and should not 'moon' the principal.

Finally, behave respectfully at graduation parties. You may not see some of these people again and it would be a shame for them to remember you acting out.

During someone else's graduation, please reply to the invitation promptly. Arrive on time, dress appropriately, and avoid yelling. Send a gift or note of congratulations if you cannot attend.

Note

- Handwrite thank you notes for graduation gifts promptly!

SPECIAL CONSIDERATIONS

Piercing

- Lip or tongue attachments at the table are not attractive.
- Think more than twice before piercing any part of your body. Always ask yourself if this is something you can live with for the rest of your life.
- *Always discuss these decisions with your parents.*

Smoking

- Not acceptable in public places and is illegal for those under 18. Smoking is very addictive and dangerous. It does not make you look cool. It just stinks.
- Vaping is *exactly* the same as cigarette smoking. Don't be fooled. And, follow the same etiquette as mentioned above.

Gum

- No popping or smacking.

Never engage in graffiti.

- This is illegal and is disrespectful of other's property.

Never litter.

- This is also illegal and is disrespectful toward all of us.

WHAT MAKES US POPULAR?

Is it important? To some of us being popular is ultimately important. Nevertheless, what is important is how you feel about yourself. Others will see you as such. Also, be a good person because that is what matters the most.

Whether or not you are popular, you need to be a good friend. To be a good friend you must be trustworthy. Don't gossip, or betray a trust. Be the type of friend that everyone knows can keep a secret. Always be loyal and stand by your friend during difficult times. Listen when she needs to talk. Be involved, be a part of your friend's life. Remember her birthday and ask questions about events she has mentioned.

Always think of those around you as special and you will be special to them.

TIME TO USE THE INFORMATION

1) Name two elevator etiquette rules.
   _____
   _____

2) What is one way we demonstrate respect in restaurants?
   _____
   _____

3) How can you be a good friend?
   _____
   _____

CHAPTER FOUR

ORGANIZATIONAL SKILLS

For those who want to gain control of their lives.

ARE YOU ORGANIZED?

Do you lose homework, toys, and phone numbers? If you said yes, this indicates that you are having problems with organizing. How about your bedroom? What does it look like? Well, the condition of your bedroom is an indication of your organizational skills. If you can't distinguish between your clean or dirty clothes, lose books, and have just plain stuff jammed under your bed, you need a little help.

The good news is that organizational skills are easy to learn and consist of easy to follow steps. We begin with checklists and move on to making sure that we are ready for each day.

ORGANIZATIONAL TOOLS

Organizing creates time and to have more time means we have control of our lives.

Checklists or to-do lists are the simplest, yet most effective organizational tool. Use checklists to write down every task you need to accomplish. Alternately, use an app, your cellphone's calendar or another similar program. Actually, I use a daily checklist built into my email program for those tasks I need to do each day and one for tasks that need to be finished later.

On your to-do list, jot down each task by importance or you could distinguish the urgent as opposed to the less urgent by letter or number. I use a star system when using a paper version of a to-do list. No kidding. I write three stars next to the urgent tasks – those jobs that must be finished promptly – while using one star for those less urgent. Today, I use colors in my email program. Both work well.

Your list could look like this:
- Don't forget to brush teeth.
- Put book bag by the door.
- Fold clean clothes and put them away.
- Study for math test.

Because you don't want to get in trouble (again) for forgetting your homework, which is in your book bag, you might write an A or 1 next to that task. Putting your clothes away may not be as important to you, so you may want to write a C or 3 next to that one. Easy, huh?

CLEAN YOUR ROOM!

Now, I'm sure your mother or father has told you at least once to "Clean your room!" What does 'clean your room' mean anyway? Does it mean to go into your room with a bottle of Windex and paper towels and start spraying and wiping?

Clean-your-room is actually a group of separate tasks, as is the same with many other jobs. You may have to make your bed – with no clothes under the sheets – pick up all of the dirty clothes, put them into the dirty clothesbasket, and put all of your books on your bookshelf. Alternatively, you may have a long list of tasks to do.

One of my best friends has a daughter who always had the messiest room and just couldn't clean it per her mother's expectations. At the age of twelve, she decided that it would be easier for her to write down all of the tasks she needed to do in order to get her room in the best possible condition.

Therefore, she went around her room noting everything that needed attention. She noted that her clean clothes needed to be put away. Before that, however, she needed to clean her drawers. She needed to put her books away. However, she couldn't do that because her book shelves were messy. She found that there were many tasks like this.

Her solution was simple. She wrote down all of those tasks that must be done before she could actually clean her room. Then, she took her scissors and cut the paper so that each task was on a separate strip of paper. She put all into a bowl, stirred it up, and chose one task. This is how she started to *clean her room.*

When a big job seems too large for you, this is a simple, yet effective solution. It can be fun too!

Note:
- Make a **checklist for items you take to school** every day and post it on your door.

ACADEMIC PLANNERS AND NOTEBOOKS

Use an academic planner or other notebook to list homework assignments and projects. Many schools have planners for sale that are very easy to use. Of course, there are apps that may accomplish this task as well.

Let's say that you have a test in Math on Tuesday, a project due this Friday, and a club meeting on Monday.

Your notebook could look like this:

The Week of May 15

Monday	Tuesday	Wednesday	Thursday	Friday
Chess club	Math test			Science project due

You could further organize these by importance and due date. The test and project are very important for your grade, so you could highlight these entries in red. While your chess club is an entertaining gathering, you could leave this as it is or highlight in a pleasant color, such as pink.

Keep your notebooks and day planners organized. Use separate sections for different classes or activities. Some schools require students to keep separate notebooks for each class. This is fine too as long as you keep them separate.

It is best to separate class notes from homework. Keep your class notes in one folder, binder or notebook. Use another folder in which to place all of your homework. However, you want to separate items that need to be finished from those that are. Therefore, once you have finished a project or homework, put it in a separate folder marked 'finished work'.

THE BIG PROJECT

This is an excellent way to use your planner, or a calendar.

If you have a big project, such as a history project break it down into smaller pieces, much as we did with the 'clean the room' project. Give yourself a timeframe in which to finish each piece.

Your planner could look like this:

The Week of May 15

Monday	Tuesday	Wednesday	Thursday	Friday
Library: book--history project	Meet with history partner		Make history project chart	

The Week of May 22

Monday	Tuesday	Wednesday	Thursday	Friday
			History project due	

STAY ORGANIZED AT HOME

What do you do with all of your returned work? You receive a huge bundle of papers every week. Not all of these have to be kept, but some do. It's best to keep reports for a while, because you may be able to use some of the information in these in the future. Keep tests, because these may help you study for future tests. Some papers your parents may wish to keep. Where will you put all of these?

Place test and returned work in files at home. A banker's box is excellent for this purpose. It is a study cardboard box with a lid. Files fit perfectly in these. File your work by month and by topic. So, place all history papers in the file marked: March—History.

For those big projects with the large maps and items that are too big for a file folder, choose a banker's box without files. Just label each project by date and topic.

For those typical homework papers, keep them until you are sure that you have credit for them. Sometimes teachers make mistakes and you might have to redo the homework. Save them in the same files as the tests and reports.

In addition, your binder gets pretty messy doesn't it? Give notes intended for your parents to them. Put your returned work where it belongs. You know where that is now. Clean up all class notes while the subject is still clear in your mind.

Clean out book bags, folders and binders at the end of the week. Take out any papers that do not belong. Discard any food left in your book bag. If you have any clothes in your bag, take them out and put them in the dirty clothes hamper.

Check your day planner or academic planner to coordinate the next week and to ensure you are on schedule. Always do this at the end of the week to guarantee that you stay within your schedule.

How will you remember to check your day planner for next week's schedule?

MASTER CALENDAR

Every member of the family has his own schedule, his appointments, activities, clubs, and obligations. How can we coordinate our schedule successfully without knowing what everyone else in the household is doing?

Just consider if you are working on a science project and need to go to the library, which is a few miles away from your home. You make plans to meet your science partner Friday afternoon to look for the perfect book. However, on Friday you discover that you have no ride. Everyone in the home who drives has other commitments. It would have been nice to know sooner wouldn't it?

Create a master calendar that lists everyone's activities and commitments that affect you. A master calendar is simply a calendar that is accessible to everyone in the household. Many people put these on the refrigerator, on the inside of a cabinet, or in a kitchen drawer. Actually, a new trend is for everyone to use their on-line computer calendar to keep tract of each other.

On your calendar: list holidays, birthdays, parent's anniversaries (neither will drive you anywhere on their anniversary) and major events. Note exams and due dates for projects. Don't forget any club or sports activity.

Note:

Cellphone calendars can also be used for this task.

SCHEDULE YOUR TIME

In order to be in control of our time, we must create a schedule. Schedule regular times for dinner, bedtime, and create time periods for specific activities like television, games and visiting. You will be amazed at how little time you actually have to work with during the school year.

Take for example you get up at 6 am and you go to school at 7:15. School begins at 7:45 and ends at 3:15. You get home at 3:45 and do your homework until 5:30, have one-half of an hour to play games, and have dinner at 6 pm.

Do you have the rest of the evening to yourself? Probably not, because we didn't factor in club or sports, trips to the library, tutors, after school classes and interaction with family.

Your schedule could look like this:

6 am: rise, bathe, breakfast	3 pm: school ends
7 am: leave for school	3:15-4 pm: homework
8 – 11 am: class	5- 6 pm: baseball practice
12 pm: lunch	7 pm: dinner
1 pm: free period--library	8 pm: homework
2 pm: class	9 pm: bed

WHERE DO YOU WORK? WHEN?

Designate a space for work and schedule a time for it. A person needs three things in order to study well. Those three things are, light, quiet, and a smooth surface to use. We cannot study with music or noise and we need adequate light and preferably a desk.

Many of us work in the kitchen. There is plenty of light, a table to work on, and as long as your brothers and sisters are quiet, it is relatively quiet.

When working, do nothing else. Many people think that they can work for 10 minutes and play a game for 10 minutes. No way. No one can keep his train of thought to do an assignment correctly with frequent interruptions.

Time your breaks. You would be amazed to find out how much time can pass if you don't watch the clock. Work until you reach a good stopping point, and set a timer. Don't take more than a 10 minute break or you won't want to return to your assignment.

Identify subjects that are giving you trouble and work out a solution. Be honest with yourself. Ask for help.

PREPARING FOR TOMORROW

Prepare for the next day. Besides the weekly cleanup of all of your school items, clean your binder every night to make sure you are doing all your work. Throw away papers that you do not need. Put completed homework, books, and binders in your book bag and place it by the door.

Check your day planner or calendar every day for tomorrow's schedule. This will keep you from forgetting a pending test or project.

Set out clothes, shoes and other clothing choices at night. If you were to wait until morning to choose your clothing, you might find your chosen item stained. It would have been so much better to know this the night before. Check all clothes for stains, rips, and cleanliness.

GOAL SETTING

In what direction are you traveling? Are you headed in the correct direction, so you achieve everything you want? Do you even have an idea of what you want to achieve this month, this year, next year, or for your future career?

If you want to be the best player in the chess club, you will need to study the chess masters. If you eventually want to attend college, there are subjects you will need to complete today in order to reach that goal. Set goals, long and short and write them down.

Your goals could look like this:
This week:
- Get an A on my math test.

This month:
- Turn in my homework every day.

In the future:
- Go to college to be a teacher.

I hope the suggestions in this last chapter will help you to become the organized, successful person you wish to be.

TIME TO USE THE INFORMATION

1) Name the two methods for keeping track of assignments.
   _____
   _____

2) Name two methods for planning a big project.
   _____
   _____

3) What is a Master Calendar?
   _____
   _____

CHAPTER FIVE

DATING ETIQUETTE

CHANGES IN DATING ETIQUETTE

Today, dating is a *tad* different from past decades. It is appropriate for today's women to call men and invite them out for dates. Ladies may even pay. Although, I believe that gentlemen pay for at *least* the first two dates. I hope that your gentleman believes this also. Gentlemen, please note that information.

Additionally, even though some things are different, some behaviors remain the same. We treat each other with respect; men *want* to treat women as ladies and women truly *want* to be treated as ladies. I doubt that these truisms will change.

BODY LANGUAGE & BEING OUR BEST

Remember the information about body language in Chapter Two? In the non-verbal communication section, I stated that body language is particularly important in everything we do. I emphasized that it directly affects impression we project. It is all about perception.

This information is invaluable, especially when we are dating. Please review those pages.

Switching gears a bit, let's discuss the importance of attire. Since you have less than one minute to make a good impression, dressing to impress is extremely important. Every aspect of dress and behavior adds or detracts from the observer's opinion.

Visualize the Mia Thermopolis character from the movie "Princess Diaries". Not many took her seriously. Why? Her attire did not reflect her personality and future position of princess (later to be queen). Although, as soon as she changed her wardrobe, tended to her wild hair and – of course – learned to stand up straight, she did appear as a princess.

On dates, this is extremely important because your date is sizing you up, especially on *first* dates. Of course, you also want to treat your date with respect and courtesy. Honor yourself first by arriving neat and clean wearing proper attire. Respect yourself always and others will too.

Remember!

Remember to walk tall with your head up while making good eye contact. When you sit, do so with grace. Do not just flop into the chair. Sit tall with legs closed – men too – and do not slump or fidget. Keep your hands off your face, which is a sign of insecurity.

- Keep hair neat, clean, and trimmed
- Gentlemen should keep facial hair neat
- Keep fingernails clean and neatly trimmed
- Limit the cologne and perfume

CONVERSATIONAL SKILLS

Communication is essential in *all* our relationships with listening as the most important component. Intensely listen to everyone when he or she speaks. Listen attentively. Each person is important and worthy of hearing.

During a date, your conversational skills are even more important because emotions tend to run higher on a date. Each is scrutinizing every word the other person is saying.

Include others in conversations. Imagine that you are on a double date or socializing with a few friends. If you include others in the conversation and ensure that everyone is included, you will be viewed as a 'people' person—someone who is pleasurable to be with. This is a positive in the dating and relationship world.

Resist preaching. Comments such as, "Do you know how many calories are in that can of soda?" or "Reading fiction dulls the brain" is disrespectful, dismissive, and boorish.

Also, considered dismissive behavior – as if others are not as important as you are – is interrupting others. To be honest, none of us enjoys being interrupted; so we should respect others and allow them to complete their thoughts. Sometimes we become so engrossed in a conversation and bursting with ideas that we want to jump right into the middle of another's sentence. Nevertheless, we must wait our turn.

Studying current events is another very useful conversation tool. Demonstrating knowledge about events occurring locally and around the world is stimulating and interesting to others. Therefore, read your local paper; read about plays, books and events currently popular in your vicinity and the world. You will sound more interesting.

Developing common interests, demonstrates your interest in another. Study these interests so you will be better equipped to converse intelligently, helping to convey the message that you care about what is important to him or her.

Humor is an excellent conversational tool, especially during a first date. Both of you may be a bit nervous and a little humor lightens the mood. This is not something all of us can execute well. If you are not proficient in telling jokes, do not. In fact, humor is not always about telling jokes. It is observing the humorous ironies surrounding us every day. Humor should always be light, not ethnic or hurtful.

Finally, no gossiping; it breeds distrust and it is hurtful. You may just be gossiping about your date's cousin and not realize it—not the best way to end a date.

TABOO TOPICS FOR FIRST DATES

- Former loves, other dates, or past heartaches
- Money
- Sex
- Therapy or health problems

- Religion
- Politics

Homework:
- Practice your listening skills

HOW TO MEET YOUR DATE

Many times our friends are our best matchmakers. They know us, know what we like, and know what we are looking for in others. In fact, this is how my husband and I met.

A friend could arrange a meeting or introduction with someone he or she feels is that future special person. This is an effective method, as your friend can discover pertinent information about the person before you meet him/her.

If there is a special someone you have noticed, introduce yourself. There is nothing improper about being an assertive person. Most people find this refreshing.

Be aware that computer dating is very dangerous for young people.

ASKING FOR THE DATE

For a casual date, ask her/him *at least* three days in advance by telephone or in person (no texting). This is respectful behavior and demonstrates that you are not *settling* for this person because your 'real' date cancelled. If this is a special occasion, such as a wedding, ask *at least* three weeks in advance. Spur of the moment, in his or her presence, and it is an informal date, asking the last minute is fine.

Ask when she or he is not busy and in private. If you call, do so before 9 pm. A ringing phone at night is irritating to those who must wake early for work and you'd run the risk of waking the object of your affection. Be specific when asking, "Would you like to accompany me to the concert next Saturday night?" is better than, "Would you like to go out sometime soon?" Inform her/him where you would like to take her/him and when. Your date will need to know how to dress.

Go slowly on first dates. Meet for coffee, go to a game, study together or go for a walk first. There is no reason to rush. Get to know this person before jumping into a relationship.

If the Answer is Yes

- Be enthusiastic when accepting a date.
- You must keep the date

If No

- Say that you have plans if you do.
- If you want to go, but can't, be regretful.

If You Are Not Interested

- Politely decline and explain.

Don't gossip about the date you refused.

- The gossip will get back to that person and hurt him or her.

THE DATE

A NOTE TO THE MEN

The following is an example of a date at a very nice restaurant using traditional, *old fashion*, yet still in-vogue manners. Your date may be different, as is fine. Nevertheless, just try to use the manners described here in all settings. You will, most likely, be viewed as a socially-savvy gentleman.

Ask her early and inform her where you intend to take her including the time. She needs to know how to dress. Ladies view their appearance very seriously and attend to their attire with great care. So, please also compliment her on her appearance when you pick her up.

Call for a reservation at least one week in advance for a popular restaurant. Ask for a special table if you wish, as you may want a quiet setting.

Walk to her door; don't just honk your horn or text from your car. This is viewed very poorly. Offer her your arm or hand and guide her to your car. This sounds old fashion and may seem silly, but women respond positively from this type of behavior. Open and close the door for her. This is the epitome of good manners.

When you arrive at the restaurant, walk around to her side of the car, open her door and help her out of the car by offering her your hand.

Ask if she would like to check her coat if that service is available ($2 tip per coat). Give your name and time of the reservation (don't be late). Follow her as she is led to your table. Politely ask to be moved if the table is next to the kitchen or in a noisy location.

If she has worn her coat to the table, help her take it off and hand it to her. Her chair is pulled out and she sits down in the choice seat. You may sit after she is settled.

When the waiter arrives and mentions specials, ask the price if he doesn't offer it. Ask how your menu choice is cooked and of any unknown ingredients. This is more desirable than facing something you cannot eat on your plate. If something is wrong with the food or the place setting, politely ask for it to be corrected.

Remember your table manners and do not laugh if your date doesn't know how to eat something.

When the check arrives, factor a 15%-20% before-tax tip. Hold her chair and pull it out to aid her. Thank the waiter and help her into her coat.

A NOTE TO THE LADIES

Remember this section concerns an old fashion, restaurant date where he asks and you respond. Your date may be very different. Nevertheless, the behaviors are the same for all dates.

When he calls for a date and you desire to accompany him, inquire about proper attire and seem interested. Dress appropriately for the occasion. Before he sees you, ask yourself what your outfit connotes. Hot date? Be careful how you represent yourself through your attire choices.

Offer your hand when he arrives at your door, so he may walk you to his car. If he drives you to the door of the restaurant, walk inside and wait for your date by the door.

When the headwaiter greets the two of you, follow him to your table and sit in the chair he pulls out for you. Discuss the menu with your date, asking him what he is considering. It is considered impolite to order an item that is very expensive. So, order something similar to your date that costs the same or less than his order.

When the waiter arrives and mentions specials, ask the price if he doesn't offer it. Ask how your menu choice is cooked and of any unknown ingredients. This is more desirable than facing something you are allergic to on your plate. Do not laugh if your date doesn't know how to eat something. We have all faced difficult food at one time or another.

When the check arrives, excuse yourself to the restroom. Do not offer money. If there is an attendant in the restroom, leave a $.50-$1.00 tip.

Note

- Do not apply makeup at the table.

A PRIMER ON SLIDING OUT OF A CAR SEAT

Ladies, getting out of a car may be difficult when wearing a dress or skirt. However, it is not impossible. Please follow these few simple steps.

First, your date opens your door. Swing your legs around from the inside of the car to the outside, while keeping your legs together and place your feet on the ground. Push down on your seat with your left hand while holding onto the back of your seat with your right hand and lean forward. Once you are nearly out of the car, offer your hand to your date so he may guide you away from the car door. He will close the door for you.

An easy method to help your date remember that he should help you out of the car is to take a minute or so to gather your things before reaching for the car door. Usually, he will remember that he needs to assist you.

DATING DO (S) AND DON'T (S)

- Do allow the man to treat you as a lady
- Do treat her as a lady
- Do be honest, listen and ask questions
- Do know something about your date
- Do relax and be the best of yourself
- Do save the intimate moments for later
- Don't be late or judge on the first date
- Don't talk about past relationships
- Don't dominate the conversation
- Don't talk endlessly about your job
- Don't seem overly interested in money or success

IDEAS FOR A GREAT DATE

- Games—trivia, Pictionary, chess.
- Miniature golf.
- Hiking.
- Flying kites.
- Rollerblading.
- Picnics.
- Fairs.
- Going for a long walk. Both of you would have to talk, which helps get to know each other better.

BAD DATES

Parking in cars to make out, field parties, crashing a party or cruising.

Note

- Young men: She is a young lady.
    - Treat her as such.
- Young ladies: You are young ladies.
    - Behave as such.

TIME TO USE THE INFORMATION

1) Fill in the blanks.

   Every aspect of _____ and _____ adds or _____ from the observer's opinion.

2) Name three of the six "Taboo Topics" for first dates.

   _____

   _____

   _____

3) What is the best method for meeting that special person?

   _____

   _____

CHAPTER SIX

PROM ETIQUETTE

ENJOYING YOUR PROM

Picture of Kendyll and Ricky; courtesy of Natalie Sayen—Kendyll's mother.

PLANNING FOR THE PROM

Ask early. Your date will need plenty of time to prepare. Because proms have become so expensive, many couples are now sharing the costs. Therefore, if in a relationship, please discuss this option.

Arrange transportation. Many couples want a limo for this special occasion. Call for rates from several sources. You may find a variety of services and price ranges. Earn money throughout the year to pay for it and possibly share the expense with a few friends. Remember to tip the driver

If you drive, stay sober. Perhaps an older, sober friend may drive.

Note

- To save money the dinner could be at someone's house.
- Take your own pictures at the dance.

FORMAL OR SEMI-FORMAL

(Picture: Macy's website)

Formal usually means long gowns and tuxedos. Ladies should shop around. Bargains are available for those who look hard enough. There are some great discount houses for gowns. The best part is that the gowns are brand new!

Semi-formal usually means short dresses and dinner jackets or sport coats and ties. A good clothing store can show you what would be appropriate. You don't have to purchase the items there. Just learn what it is that you should wear.

Note

- If you are inviting a date from another school, let that person know what to wear.

TUXES

Tuxedos are available in all colors, but your basic black is best and is usually less expensive. This is not the time to experiment with colors. Your date may end up crying all night because you thought that it would be 'funny' to wear a purple tuxedo jacket and jeans. You can pair it with a bow tie and cummerbund.

FLOWERS

A gentleman asks his date what color her dress is and orders what the lady wants, either a wristlet, nosegay (a small bunch to carry), or corsage.

To insert the corsage, insert the pin into the fabric back up through the fabric and over the stem (about the middle of the corsage) then back through and out the fabric.

Ladies purchase a boutonniere, or small flower for her date's lapel (rose or carnation). It is usually the same color as her flowers. She pins it where the buttonhole would be on the lapel of his jacket by holding the flower in place, inserting the pin into the fabric, then up through the fabric and flower stem, back into and out of the fabric.

THE DINNER

Customarily the couple goes out to a restaurant before the prom. It does not need to be the most expensive place. You will be excited so be careful of your noise level. Remember that you are sharing this space with others. Check the bill to make sure a gratuity has not been added before tipping.

THE DANCE

Many teens just go to the dance to get their picture taken and then proceed to after dance parties. Try to stay because this is a once in a lifetime experience. Live it. Moreover, dance!

AFTER THE DANCE PARTIES

Many teens plan an after the dance party at a hotel. Be careful! Alcohol consumption is still illegal for you and can lead to an unpleasant experience. This is an important evening; please don't spoil it with such a party. Perhaps your party could be a gathering at someone's home without the alcohol.

TABLE MANNERS PRIMER

Basic manners are essential in everything we do and definitely a must at the table. The first and most important rule of the table is that we always want everyone to feel comfortable, because the essence of good manners is caring for those around us. This is the basic rule. If we keep this in mind, we will always make the right decision. Therefore, we use all of our manners like please, thank you, excuse me and please pass the... And, when someone asks for the salt, we pass the pepper as well. These travel in pairs.

RULES TO REMEMBER

- No hats at the table.
- Do not put on lipstick, clean fingernails, or comb hair at the table.
- Hold your *larger* spoon as a pencil to eat soup.
- Scoop the soup away from you.
- Use bread or knife to guide food onto your fork.
- Never place a utensil on the table after it is used.
- Everyone should have food on his plate before starting to eat.

NAPKIN RULES

- Place the napkin on the left of the place setting or on the plate if the dinner is formal.
- Place the napkin in your lap after everyone has been seated.
- If you leave the table for a moment, place the napkin to the left of the plate or on the chair.
- Blot your mouth before taking a drink.
- Place napkin to the right of the plate neatly when finished.

BREAD AND ROLLS

- Your bread plate is on your left above your forks.
- Take one piece of bread at a time.
- Put butter on your plate with the butter knife (if there is one).
- Tear one piece of bread, butter it, and eat one piece of bread at a time.

DO NOT

- Hover over your food or hold your utensils like shovels.
- Reach or blow on hot food.
- Place a utensil on the table after it is used.
- Wear any type of hat at the table.
- Make rude noises or engage in bad habits at the table.
- Lick your fingers or push food onto your fork using fingers.

For more on table manners, please read my *Table Manners* Book.

PROM REMINDERS

LADIES

Do (s)

- Do make all entrances with your date, walking next to him.
- Do dance the first and last dance with your date.
- Do go with your friends if you don't have a date.
- Do be on time.
- Do be polite.
- Do try on all clothing, accessories, and make-up well in advance.
- Do wear a wrap or shawl over a strapless dress.
- Only remove your gloves during dinner.

Don't (s)

- Don't spray hairspray anywhere other than the bathroom.
- Don't forget your date's boutonniere.
- Don't wear too much perfume.
- Don't leave your date with your friends the entire night.
- Don't use your cellphone when in his presence.
- Don't wear rings or bracelets over your gloves.

GENTLEMEN

Do (s)

- Do pull out a ladies chair for her.
- Do stand when a lady stands to excuse herself.
- Do escort your lady whenever appropriate and make all entrances with her.
- Do escort your date to her door step at the end of the night.

Don't (s)

- Don't be late or forget your wallet.
- Don't seat yourself while a lady is standing.
- Don't drink and drive.
- Don't enter a room before a lady.
- Don't forget her corsage.
- Don't wear too much cologne.
- Don't leave your date with your friends the entire night.
- Don't use your cellphone when in her presence.

GENTLEMEN AND LADIES

- Compliment each other.
- Don't chew gum.
- Don't break up with your date that day.

FREQUENTLY ASKED QUESTIONS

When should I ask my date to the prom?

- Ask your date two months before the prom. This is plenty of time to shop and prepare.

May young ladies ask young men out to the prom?

- Traditionally, the young man would ask a young lady to the prom. While ladies may ask a young man in these modern times, it is best to follow tradition.

Who pays?

- Typically, the young man pays if he can afford it. However, some couples split the cost.

May I go to the prom by myself, or may I go with a group of friends?

- Sure, you may go with a group of friends. This is a great idea, because you can share the cost of travel. Nevertheless, you shouldn't go alone because you will want to dance.

TIME TO USE THE INFORMATION

1) What is the difference between "Formal and Semi-Formal" attire?

   _____

   _____

2) What are the two "Glove Etiquette" rules mentioned in this chapter?

   _____

   _____

3) Where would you find your "Bread Plate" on a table?

   _____

   _____

CHAPTER SEVEN

BUSINESS ETIQUETTE

WHERE TO BEGIN?

Have you worked outside the home before? Do you presently retain a paying job?

If you do not have a paying job as of now, consider your hobbies and all the activities in which you are proficient. Lawn mowing could develop into a job with a landscaping service and baby-sitting could become a job with a summer camp or a children's service with the city parks and recreation department. Consider all of your skills, talk to parents, network with friends and businesses that you frequent, talk to your school counselor, and check the classifieds and bulletin boards.

HOW TO ACQUIRE THE JOB

You may have to create a **resume**. Many computer programs contain templates to help you. Yours should contain this information.

RESUME INFORMATION

- Name, address, telephone number
- Education: diplomas, certificates, last grade completed
- Honors or awards you received in school
- Courses related to the job for which you are applying
- Interests and hobbies, only if pertinent to the job you're seeking
- Past work experience
- Names, addresses, and phone numbers of three people who would be willing to provide references
- You may choose from previous employers, members of the clergy, teachers, and family friends, but before listing them, you must get their permission
- Family members should not be listed as references

FILLING OUT APPLICATIONS

Pick up more than one copy of the application for each job you wish to apply. Read the applications fully before filling each out. This way you can make any mistakes on the rough draft. The final copy should be error free and neat.

Of course, many employers have applications online these days. This simplifies matters quite a bit. Just make sure your spelling and grammar is perfect.

SETTING UP THE INTERVIEW

Some businesses conduct interviews on specific days. Note when these days are and how to sign up. You may have to call for an interview. Know what you want to say before you make the call.

THE INTERVIEW

Dress appropriately with attention to hygiene, attending to clothing, hair and nails. Choose clothing that is slightly dressier than the clothing current employees are wearing.

Ladies beware of wearing too much makeup. Moreover, *everyone* should be cautious about cologne.

Be on time. Report to the receptionist or the person who greets you and wait quietly.

Take your resume and your application if you haven't submitted it as yet. Bring proof of citizenship if you are not a United States citizen and your Social Security number.

Take your manners. Smile and shake hands when your interviewer extends his or her hand. You don't want to seem too eager. Stand until asked to sit; the seat is not yours until it is offered to you. Do not chew gum, smoke, or fidget. Most importantly, leave the cellphone at home! If your cellphone rings during an interview, you have just lost that opportunity.

BE PREPARED

To be better prepared for questions research the business before your interview.

The interviewer leads the conversation. When it is your turn to speak, ask questions about the training program, opportunities for advancement, and the work that you will be doing. Do not ask about salary or benefits until you are sure that you have the job.

Please Remember

- Remain calm.
- Be aware of your body language.
- Sit straight.
- Don't swing legs.
- Maintain good eye contact.

BE HONEST

Do not lie about anything; it will be discovered, and you may be fired.

THANK THE INTERVIEWER

Send a thank you note for the person's kindness and the opportunity to interview.

ONCE YOU HAVE THE JOB

Focus on your hygiene. Arrive to work clean every day with teeth and hair brushed, wearing clean pressed clothes.

No grooming at your desk where others may see you. Use the restroom to brush your hair, pick your teeth, and to shave—although you should have shaved at home. Remember the old phrase, "*A time and place for everything.*"

Casual Fridays seem to have become everyday work clothes for many. Nevertheless, we are still expected to dress appropriately. We should always dress for our positions with a nod to the next promotion.

Ladies must be especially careful. When we allow our bodies to *speak* for us our message is not what we had intended. Consequently, dressing conservatively – no cleavage – is vitally important. To the point, dress well to be taken seriously!

CONSIDERATIONS

Avoid stomach revealing, tight fitting tops, short skirts, shorts and flip-flops.

Avoid pants that do not fit properly.

Clothing and appearance must reflect your position, or the position you wish to have.

You may be the first, and in some cases, the only person your customers will see. Your appearance reflects upon the entire organization.

Always ask yourself how you would appear to your customers.

Project a professional image always.

DIFFICULT SITUATIONS

How you handle difficult people is very important, like those obnoxious people who pull in front of you on the freeway and that person who tries to sneak in front of you when you've been standing in line for an hour. However, in the workplace, you need razor sharp coping skills.

How do you deal with difficult people? It isn't always easy. Yet, the key to solving conflicts is simply willingness. We have to *want* to resolve the problem.

When you are faced with an angry, venting person, never lose control. Request back up if necessary. Give the angry person physical space and time to vent; step back and listen. Allow him or her to rant as long as he or she is not abusive. When the person is finished, ask what you can do to resolve the problem. If you cannot resolve the problem, state that you will find someone who can.

Note

- Never state that this is not your job.

HONESTY AND INTEGRITY

"Honesty pays, but it doesn't seem to pay enough to suit some people." F.M. Hubbard

Honesty is imperative in the workplace; in fact, it is imperative in everything we do. I believe that most everyone wants to be honest and feels as if he is. However there is a quirky disconnect in a number of employee's thoughts about what is and what is not dishonest.

Recently, I was having a delightful conversation with the owner of a local coffee shop. As I sipped, she was lamenting about her experiences trying to find employees. Her last attempt felt that it was appropriate to make complimentary, special coffees for his friends. When she confronted him, the surprised young man stated that he wanted to please the customers. Of course, for her it meant lost sales.

As she was interviewing another potential, he stated that his last job was great because he worked for a major coffee house and drank as much coffee as he wanted. When she asked how much coffee cost him while working there, he stated, "Why should I pay, they are a large corporation; it doesn't cost them anything." Hmmm….

A company is owned and run by *people*. When you or I take things, even a paper clip, it is stealing. When we lie about our past, we are lying to people. When we take credit for someone else's idea, we are dishonest. The principles we live by every day and in every situation is what defines us as human beings. Please remember your values.

Note

- When we take credit for someone else's idea, it is dishonest and unethical.
- A company is owned and run by people.

"Where is there dignity unless there is honesty?" Marcus Tullius Cicero

OFFICE POLITICS

If you want to be effective and make your job easier, you will need to **interact** with those from all levels of the organization and they will interact with you. Therefore, the positive side of office politics could be that we all realize that the best way to get something from anyone is for them to want to help you.

Nevertheless, why would anyone want to drop what he is doing to help you? Well, if you want a person's expert help, you will need to be equally available when that person needs help from you. It is usually reciprocal; most of the time you will get back what you give out. It is only human nature.

Yet, if we use our position to attempt to **power over** others instead of remembering to treat others with respect, we will achieve nothing.

Please consider this true story. One of my dearest friends is a manager in a professional setting. He has excellent manners and knows to treat others with respect. His office is next to his director's office, so he can hear other managers stomping into the director's office demanding to see the director at that very moment. More often than not, they were not allowed. Alternately, my friend walks into the director's office, asks the director's assistant politely, using her name, and is most often given an appointment that day. Could it be that simple manners are that powerful? You bet.

You will need to build trusted, helpful relationships with those below, at and above your level, so in turn and in time they will assist you. Every day you will need to work on these relationships, remembering to treat others as you wish to be treated. This is our **personal power**, a choice and knowledge of how to treat others.

NEGATIVE OFFICE POLITICS

Eventually, no matter where you work or position you hold you will experience gossip, name-calling, and just plain negative office politics.

When you listen to those who gossip, you are engaging in the activity. Therefore, inform the gossiper that you don't want to hear anything negative, because you work with this person. Gossip breeds distrust. Do not allow the chatter to spread.

People believe what they hear and soon the victim of gossip is eating her lunch alone and looking for another job.

I have a very good friend who experienced this vindictive behavior recently. My friend is the newest employee in her office, while most of the others have been there for many years. She was hired to modify existing programs and to create new ones, which generated anxiety. Many are not comfortable with change, so soon the gossip began.

My friend is a strong young woman who realized what was happening. She was crushed when she received her evaluation saying that *she* cannot work well with others or alone. Taking a deep breath she politely challenged the evaluation and looked for another job.

Who knows why these things happen. I relayed this story to another close friend to try to get some answers for myself. Of course, I used no names. She is twenty years older than my young friend and yet told a very similar story. The same thing happened to her in a law office twenty years ago. She left her position also. This is the power of gossip.

So you see this is a destructive force, which can and will cause good workers to leave. Businesses lose money every year in employee turnover. To train new employees for the same position repeatedly is costly.

Also, think twice about confiding too much in your coworker. Office relationships can be very fragile and could fail. Often, we rush into relationships with others in our office before realizing exactly who this person is. And then, we find that we have told the office snoop how much we dislike our boss.

This brings up another absolute no-no. Please avoid negative chatter about your company or superiors. It is bad for morale and for you. You may find yourself scrambling to find a new job.

Please Consider

- Your coworkers are also your customers; provide respectful service.

- Listen attentively to customers and coworkers.
- Communicate clearly without slang, euphemisms, or vulgarities.
- Build trusted, helpful relationships with everyone.
- Just say no to negative office politics: gossip, negative chatter, and harassment.
- Assist others; they will usually reciprocate in kind.
- Avoid negative chatter and criticizing others.

NETIQUETTE

Nearly everyone uses email and the Internet at work these days. However, many are not using their best manners or common sense.

Netiquette, according to Encarta Online is defined as a set of empirically derived rules for getting along harmoniously in the electronic communication environment. I will not mention all the rules, for there are many and you have access to all of them on the web. However, we need to discuss using the computer and all of its tools politely.

First, remember that every rule we follow in the workplace also refers to email and our visits online. Never engage in hate mongering, which includes all ethnicities, religions, ages, sexual orientation, cultures, and genders. Of course, sexually explicit sites are off limits. In addition, spending valuable work time online for personal use is not appropriate, as would be excessive phone use. Moreover, avoid swearing, offensive language and harassment in email.

Secondly, style is as essential when composing email messages as it is with writing your business letter. Grammar, spelling, tone, and attention to the reader of the document are what we strive for in our business letters. And yet, we send emails with all capitals, which appear to the reader as if we are yelling. In addition, notes with acronyms like OYOT (on your own time) may be difficult for the reader to decode.

In addition, there is no body language in emails. So, refrain from humor and sarcasm, which can be misunderstood.

Email is as permanent as any other written document we write. Just hitting the delete key does not mean it is removed from the depths of the hard drive. Anyone may read what you write. Once sent, it may be copied and circulated and it has your return address.

Please Consider

- Reread your messages before hitting send.
- Keep your emails short.
- Did you forget the attachment? Bad mistake.
- No sarcastic humor, all caps, or acronyms.
- Use clear subject lines.
- Double-check the recipient.
- Don't forward someone's message without permission.
- Do not forward jokes.
- Don't write when you're angry. It is called flaming.
- Check your email accounts often and reply promptly.
- Never write anything that you would not want posted on a bulletin board.

BECOME AN ENTREPRENEUR

Perhaps you're already doing a job or engaging in a hobby that can translate into a real business. Consider these business ideas!

Of course, it's best to check with parents first.

- Gardening service, baby-sitting, or delivering newspapers
- Create a newsletter about the neighborhood—sell ads to local businesses
- Services to the elderly, such as reading, writing letters, or running errands
- Pet sitter
- Repair items you know how to repair

- Vehicle detailing—wash, clean the inside and wax
- Baking for special occasions
- Disc jockey
- Party planner
- Small painting jobs—fence, doghouse
- Gift-wrapping service
- Ironing
- House sitting
- Errand service
- Ask your parents before starting any of these services

"Just follow good old fashioned, proper behavior and you can't go wrong." Charlotte Ford

TIME TO USE THE INFORMATION

1) Name three items you should list on a resume.

_____
_____
_____

2) Fill in the blanks.

Yet, if we use our _____ to attempt to _____ _____ others instead of remembering to treat others with _____, we will achieve nothing.

3) What is the number one rule of netiquette?

_____
_____

ANSWERS TO QUIZ QUESTIONS

CHAPTER ONE

1) What could you do to help more around the house?

Suggestions:

- Help with the laundry
- Care for the pets
- Perform yardwork
- Clean the garage
- Do the dishes
- Cook dinner

2) How will you ensure you are safe when away from the house?

Suggestions:

- Carry a house key
- Charge your cell phone
- Take new medications only when a parent is present
- Do not walk home alone after dark

3) How can you be a better host to guests?

Suggestions:

- Inform your guests of the house rules
- Plan activities
- Offer refreshments

Chapter Two

1) **What would you wear to a nice restaurant?**

Did you take into consideration the location? If dining at a restaurant in New York, your attire would be much more formal than if dining in a small town in California.

Suggestions:

Typically, young men could wear slacks and a nice shirt. For a more formal location, this could include a jacket or suit and tie.

Typically, young ladies could wear slacks and a nice blouse or a dress. For a more formal location, this could include a jacket.

2) How will you begin a conversation?

Suggestions:

- Start with the information given to you
- Mention **music** playing in the background

3) How will you use a cellphone politely?

Suggestions:

- Do not use a cellphone while in the company of another
- Do not use a cellphone in a restaurant, place of worship or theater

CHAPTER THREE

1) Name two elevator etiquette rules.

Suggestions:

    If it is not crowded, women and girls enter and leave first

    However, if there are elderly onboard, we give those much older than ourselves respect by allowing them to enter and exit first

2) What is one way we demonstrate respect in restaurants?

Suggestions:

    Treat waitstaff with the respect; they are people, not just fixtures.

    A reservation at a restaurant is a promise of arrival, so, punctuality is paramount.

3) How can you be a good friend?

Suggestions:

    Don't gossip, or betray a trust

    Always be loyal and stand by your friend during difficult times

    Be involved; be a part of your friend's life

CHAPTER FOUR

1) **Name the two methods for keeping track of assignments.**

    Use a physical paper planner or electronically, using an app or computer program

2) **Name two methods for planning a big project.**

> Break it down into smaller projects using a planner or an electronic device.

3) **What is a Master Calendar?**

> It is a calendar used to keep track of all family member's schedules. This can be a paper calendar or an electronic version.

CHAPTER FIVE

1) **Fill in the blanks.**

- Every aspect of <u>dress</u> and <u>behavior</u> adds or <u>detracts</u> from the observer's opinion.

2) **Name three of the six "Taboo Topics" for first dates.**

Suggestions:

- Former loves, other dates, or past heartaches
- Money
- Sex
- Therapy or health problems
- Religion or Politics

3) **What is the best method for meeting that special person?**

- Meeting your future date through a friend is best.

Chapter Six

1) **What is the difference between "Formal and Semi-Formal" attire?**
   - Formal usually means long gowns and tuxedos.
   - Semi-formal usually means short dresses and dinner jackets or sport coats and ties.

2) **What are the two "Glove Etiquette" rules mentioned in this chapter?**
   - Don't wear rings or bracelets over your gloves.
   - Only remove your gloves during dinner.

3) **Where would you find your "Bread Plate" on a table?**
   - It is on your left directly above your forks.

Chapter Seven

1) **Name three items you should list on a resume.**

Suggestions:
   - Name, address, telephone number
   - Education: diplomas, certificates, last grade completed
   - Honors or awards you received in school
   - Courses related to the job for which you are applying
   - Interests and hobbies, only if pertinent to the job you're seeking
   - Past work experience

2) Fill in the blanks.

- Yet, if we use our <u>position</u> to attempt to **power over** others instead of remembering to treat others with <u>respect</u>, we will achieve nothing.

3) **What is the number one rule of netiquette?**

- Every rule we follow in the workplace also refers to email and our visits online.

YOUR AUTHOR

Your author, Rebecca Black, also known as The Polite One, recently retired from her company **Etiquette Now!** after a successful and rewarding 20+ years. As the owner and facilitator of her company, this retired elementary school teacher designed and presented custom etiquette workshops for the individual, corporate, governmental and educational client. Due to her extensive knowledge of the subject, she is also a well-respected author of etiquette books and lesson plans.

Considered an expert in the field, Rebecca answers etiquette questions (Q & A) and offers advice through her blogs: Got Etiquette Advice, Got Wedding Etiquette, and The Polite One's Insights.

Although for many years, Rebecca, focused her writing on etiquette issues, she is currently following her passion of writing fiction. A few of her most recent children's books also focus on the environment: *Save the Jellywonkers: Help Keep The Oceans Clean; Beware the Blackness, A Jellywonker Adventure;* and *The Tale of a Bear & Pony: A Yellowstone Adventure*

Please visit rebeccablackauthor.blogspot.com for more information about Rebecca's current news.

Connect with Us
https://www.facebook.com/ThePoliteOne
https://www.facebook.com/rebeccablackauthor/

Visit Us
Rebecca Black Author

Etiquette Now! Insights

Got Etiquette Advice

Got Wedding Etiquette

Living Well & Enjoying Life—Rebecca Style

The Polite One's Insights

The Polite Traveler

https://www.amazon.com/author/rebecca_black

Published Fiction Books by Rebecca Black
The Tale of a Bear & Pony; A Yellowstone Adventure

Save The Jellywonkers! -- Help Keep Our Oceans Clean

Beware the Blackness! A Jellywonker Adventure

Sapphire and the Atlantians

War in Atlantis

The Return of the Tui Suri

Published Etiquette Books by Rebecca Black

Dining Etiquette: Essential Guide for Table Manners, Business Meals, Sushi, Wine and Tea Etiquette

Dress for All Occasions—The Basics, Attire Must-Haves, Dress Code Definitions & FAQs

Entertaining Skills 101

Etiquette for The Socially Savvy Adult: Life Skills for All Situations

Etiquette for the Socially Savvy Teen: Life Skills for All Situations

Golf Etiquette: Civility on the Course

How to Tea: British Tea Times

How to Teach Your Children Manners: Essential Life Skills Your Child Needs to Know!

International Business Travel Etiquette: Seal the Deal by Understanding Proper Protocol

Navigating Important Events Without Appearing Clueless: Common sense advice, historical reflection and gift-giving savvy

Reach Your Potential: A guide to help you achieve your goals, be happier, and find your path

Societal Rage: Problem solving for our increasingly violent world

Sushi Etiquette: The guide for those who wish to eat sushi properly and avoid insulting the chef

Train the Trainer Guide: The essential guide for those who wish to present workshops and classes for adults

Wedding & Reception Planning: The Etiquette Guide for Planning the Perfect Wedding

Wine Etiquette--From holding the glass to ordering a bottle of wine in a restaurant and everything in-between

Workplace Etiquette: How to Create a Civil Workplace

Published Lesson Plans

Business Meal Etiquette

Career Fair Etiquette

Entertaining Skills 101: Lesson Plans for Those Who Wish to Present Workshops

Etiquette for the Socially Savvy Teen

Golf Etiquette

Growing Up Socially Savvy

How to Become a Socially Savvy Lady

How to Tea; British Tea Times

How to Teach Your Children Manners

Just for Teens, Skills for the Socially Savvy

Manners for Children

Organizational Skills

Prom Etiquette

Proper Business Attire

Skills for the Socially Savvy and Well-Dressed Teen

Skills for the Socially Savvy and Well-Organized Teen

Table Manners

Train the Trainer

Wine Etiquette

Workplace Etiquette

Wedding Lesson Plans

Lessons for the Newly Engaged

Wedding Planning

Wedding Reception Planning

Please visit https://www.amazon.com/author/rebecca_black for information about collecting more etiquette books.

Made in the USA
Las Vegas, NV
08 February 2024

85499109R00083